It's Fun to Be One!

Written by Heather Bruhl

Illustrated by Geraldine Aikman

Copyright @ 2016
It's Fun to Be One!
Written by Heather Bruhl
Published by Longwood Publishing
www.longwoodpublishing.com

Illustrations and Graphic Design by Geraldine Aikman
www.aikmandesign.com

ISBN 978-0692734780
ISBN 0692734783

I dedicate this book to all new parents.
God chose you and gave you the gift
of a newborn baby.
May you cherish them always
and provide a safe and loving home
in your heart.

~ Heather Bruhl

I joyfully arrive
with welcoming wishes.
Daddy showers me
with warm tender kisses.

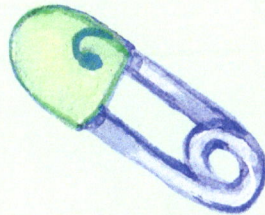

I Love You

Wrapped in blankies
of pink and blue
and monogrammed hankies
saying I Love You.

Readied bottles
of nice warm milk,
my skin is soft
and smooth as silk.

I listen to Mommy
sweetly singing,
she holds me gently
while softly swinging.

My eyes close slowly
as I start to drift
and Mommy unwraps
a baby gift.

It's Fun to Be One !

I drool a little
while taking a nap,
and feel the warmth
of my newly knit cap.

We go for a walk
inside my stroller,
the world passes by
as I grow older.

People stop
to admire me,
my bright blue eyes
still trying to see.

Precious tiny
little girls,
hair adorned
with soft fine curls.

And big and bouncy
baby boys
who carry around
cute animal toys.

one

one

It's Fun to Be One !

one

ONE

Bath time playing
with rubber ducks,
sometimes dollies,
sometimes trucks.

I splash about
in bubbles and suds
waiting for
my tummy rubs.

Sitting and cooing
in my wooden cradle,
my tiny fingers
explore my navel.

They dress me up
in cozy jammies,
I am nurtured by
my loving nannies.

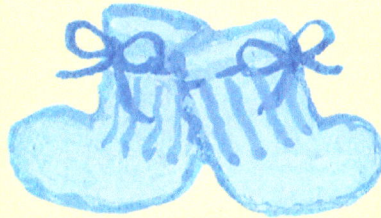

I snuggle deeply
inside my bed,
Daddy gently
caresses my head.

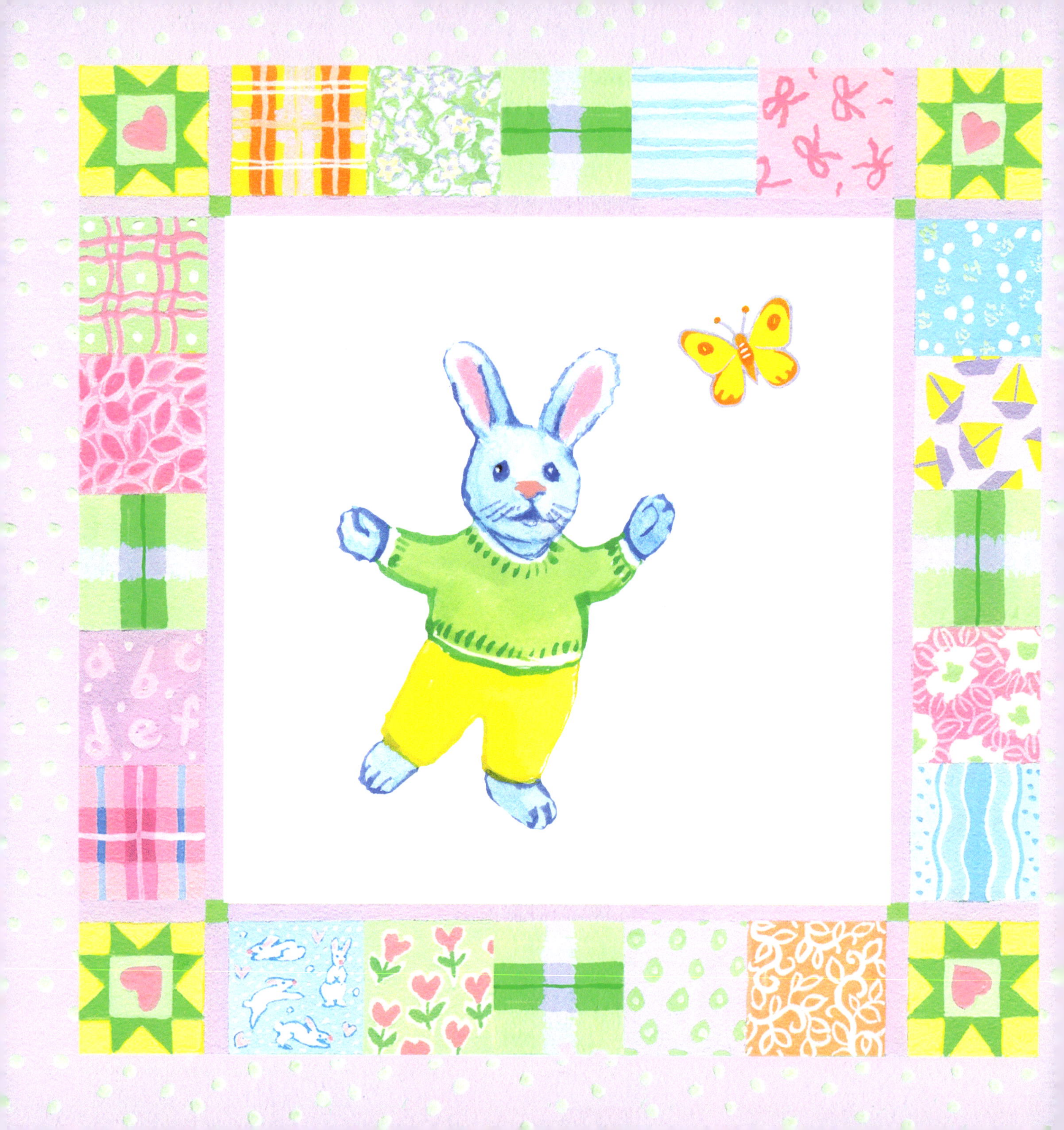
a b c
d e f

It's Fun to Be One !

Lullabies play
inside my head,
as I get ready
to go to bed.

Lambs and ducks
and bunnies and sheep,
all waiting for me
to fall asleep.

Warm and pink
is my cute nose,
I stretch out long
and curl my toes.

I enjoy my time
in my cradle rocking,
I get to see
my Christmas stocking.

I'm Mommy and Daddy's
love and affection.
I'm a newborn baby…
I'm pure perfection.

baby 🩷 baby

It's Fun to Be One !

1

www.ingramcontent.com/pod-product-compliance
Lightning Source LLC
LaVergne TN
LVHW072053070426
835508LV00002B/72